Praise for *Evelyn As*

Christine Butterworth-McDermott's *Evelyn As* is a vivid, poetic account of the early life and career of late 19th and early 20th Century chorus girl, artists' model, and actress Evelyn Nesbit. These dynamic, fraught, and textural poems provide a stunning and heartbreaking portrait of a life of stardom, violence, scandal, and survival, weaving together everything from the Persephone myth and Little Red Riding Hood to Rapunzel and Snow White—not to mention also gaze theory, the sometimes (wildly complicated) transformative power of art, and the roles we all play both willingly and un-. At its heart, *Evelyn As* is a compelling, gripping, and tragic blockbuster of a book, simultaneously cinematic, awe inspiring, and crushing.
—Matt Hart

In these poems, Butterworth-McDermott undoes the red velvet cloaks, rolls up the bear rugs, and dismantles the swings that made the child model, Evelyn Nesbit, famous. We see past the blinding lights of Stanford White's photography bulbs to Evelyn as a young girl trapped in a system of nightmarish power. Telling her story through the lens of famous figures that include Persephone, Little Red Riding Hood, and Scheherazade, *Evelyn As* connects a long line of nightmarish narratives together. In the process, Butterworth-McDermott's poems slash through centuries of female objectification.
—Julie Babcock

Evelyn As is a timely and timeless tale told by a speaker who weaves myth and fairytale to retrace the many forked paths of Nesbit's life. This collection offers a moving apology to a girl who lost her girlhood to the overindulgence of many adults around her. In portrait after portrait, Butterworth-McDermott documents Nesbit's early life in searing detail, moving the poet's sympathy

and ire and her desire to unwind the past. As she writes in the book's incantatory final line: "may everything done be undone."
–Jen McClanaghan

The Spellbook *of* Fruit & Flowers

Christine Butterworth-McDermott

Fomite
Burlington, VT

ISBN-978-1-953236-80-7
Library of Congress Control Number: 2023934263

Fomite
58 Peru Street
Burlington, VT 05401
www.fomitepress.com

03/09/2023

*for all the girls who reminded me that not
all the flowers in the garden
are poison*

*and for Cornelia,
the strongest woman I have ever known*

Contents

I.

II.

III.

All these things must come to the soul from
its roots, from where it is planted. The tree
that is beside the running water is fresher and
gives more fruit
    —*St. Teresa of Avila*

Mistress Mary, Quite contrary,
How does your garden grow?
With Silver Bells, And Cockle Shells,
And so my garden grows.
    —*Tommy Thumb's Pretty Song Book*

I.

I Hear You're Sick of Pomegranates

You're lying. Desire is just dormant.
The fruit, a globe easily pierced, is open
                and splayed for you — red flesh
        peeled back, an untoggled coat,

the smallest bead a metaphor for how we cluster
        around the core of life, clinging
        to tenuous fibers, shoulder to shoulder
with fragile comrades.

I suspect, that in the past, you've sucked juice
                out each gemlike seed, your mouth
        pursed in pleasure. You enjoyed it
when there were bowls, full.

        Only now do you curse all
the effort. What you really hate is the reminder
                that there were no apples in Eden —
        history and topography don't correlate:
North America, the Middle East.
And it has made you bitter
                to know pomegranates led you here,
to this loneliness, to this knowledge
                that you are not some God.

You liked to think the tree, the roots, the fruit
        were all yours, rather than some lucky
                design, a bright supernatural gift,

but now as you hold it, orb to palm,
you know your own coat
        must be thrown back, your own life broken
open and plucked, bit into,

        let go   discarded,
            falling to earth.

Seeds and blood cannot be contained.
        You know that—even as you use
such empty words as tiresome, familiar,
    predictable. You know that you would take

the fruit greedily, piece by piece,
            and devour it,
            if it were only offered by some soft hand.

Here is the Green Apple

Here is me, here is you —

if we get down to this rot, to the worm,
do we watch it morph to serpent?

If we get down to the core,
would you plant the seeds or throat

their poison? Here is the tree, forbidden.

we slither each time we bite
and hold sweet flesh on tongues, dancing
around cyanide.

I cannot make you less Adam, me less Eve
so here is the end:

swallow the seed, swallow the seed.

Spell for Attraction, Containing Belladonna

Your eyes are familiar: purple like the skin
of a fruit she's bitten—

In another life, this girl addressed you
and undressed you without hesitation

but in this one, she rocks her loneliness
until the Fates grant her some unwinding.

The spell says first she must dig

        in the black
        dirt,   pull up
        the nightshade,
        replace it

bread   *salt*   *brandy*

        let the hole
        devour
        these gifts

then shovel the dirt back over, bury
that which she offers up.

The spell says she must trek
for home, moist ground mucking up
her shoes. The spell says she must
not speak on the way across the field.

She must not speak until the hearth
greets her. Then she may think how

both now must be joined. The spell says
to grind the leaves, boil them down,

drop that tea in the eyes.
The spell promises they will grow wide

and beautiful—*bella donna*
—she will blink the power

 of the root. The spell says
you will not be able to look away.

If You Were To Change Me Into Flower

If you were to change me into flower,
blossom me open.

Let me radiate as poppy—
      I cannot hothouse
dance under closed glass.
        I cannot rose or orchid.

If you were to change me give me
common ground.

Let my dark eye remain open,
      ever aware despite harsh
sun. And at the dim of dusk, let me
      umbrella-down.

It would be enough to lay under a field of stars.
It would be enough to be brushed
      by your tanned cheek.

It would be enough to swell against your lips
in their last whispered prayer
      before falling, plucked.

The Sugared Plum

According to tradition,
it's bad luck to refuse your kiss
under the mistletoe.

Six drupes means six times
the tip of your tongue should hover
in the innermost corner

of my mouth. And though I am
curious about the taste
your lips might bring,

I also wonder how many tainted
berries brought you to linger
here, with the likes of me.

How many presents have you
already unwrapped, how often
have your fingers folded back paper

—or choked up girls with ribbon?
I'd like to stand here—instead—
on the threshold of your potential

gifts, rather than sweat in stifling rooms,
heady on spice and wool,
tradition hanging down above us.

Maybe later you can pull me out
to where the crisp air cools this blush.
Maybe later, it will be enough

to stare together at houses that shine
like beacons sugared with snow.
And then, if you lay your hand

to my throat—then, under no eaves
or fabrication, it may be just
enough to close our eyes, to wait,

to hold still.

Wallflower/Clubroot

Just let me	*	come
vine	Over	baby
here	*	see
the water	*	come in
that's needed	*	it's fine
almost within	*	reach
reach	*	there's a dance
I can't	move	we could do
there's	*	here
no sustenance for	*	unfold
	*	those pent up
my leaves	*	limbs, lover
I know your kind	*	come on, baby
no amount of	*	I've got
	water	enough
is enough	*	hold out
I'll hold out	*	your tongue

Spell for Resistance, with Tansy

Life circles around imaginings.
You like to play Hedylogos, offering
tussie-mussie of sweet and talk,
sweet and tart, just enough to strum
a string in my body, not my heartbeat.
Or perhaps it's Pan you admire,
all pipe and play. Anyway, like Syringa,
I'll keep hiding lilacs and tansy in my hair,
and mince my steps between here and there,
among the flowering quince. I'm out
of your reach but that doesn't mean
I don't glance back at you standing there.
How you're wanting. And I'm a sucker
for the peaches you offer. I'm a sucker
for juice. Later, crown removed, I'll offer
you the dying blooms to ground as fuel
for your bee smoker. Isn't that what
we all hope to do, mesmerize by smoke?
I'll add a bit more each time to coax you
past this buzzing dance of insistence.

Sale Pending

I have thought of you that way since the moment
when framed in the dark doorway, you came
toward me, after I had put the key in the lock
and stepped into the empty house. What was it
that pushed me forward to brush your shoulder
as I led you through drafty room after room,
the gold ring on your finger signifying nothing
but a pretty token of what you were telling me
was broken and must be fixed. We stood
in a room without a bed and I was
almost undone by the thrum of your body,
the hum of its electrical charge. To kiss you
would be to lick a socket, rocket hard to disaster.
I search for a bomb shelter, some way out
of here, some safe room — but you stand
grinning, hands out, asking
about the flowered wallpaper, the soft
carpet you would lay down upon the floor.

Datura Innoxia

You're showy at night when the rest
of the world sleeps. That's when you knock on
the window of my chest, and suggest
I let you in—but I know what those white folds

hold, been there, done the tease
of your delirium, I know the friction of your cold
white kisses and the empty bed in the morning,
how closed up you get. I am well aware

that this is superficial, this is a storming
of quick back petalling to nothing rooted.
How I'd rather you haruspex me open
at the softest place between my ribs, flap

my skin like a white elephant ear, or a crescent.
There must be *something* there to see, drag it out,
and lay my organs in threes, realign
and reconstruct me. God, you prick

at me when I desire to get inside to the seeds.
You make me bleed. And whatever this may be,
your agitation, confusion, hallucination—I don't
know—but my heart rate climbs anyway.

Hot and flushed, my vision blurs. My mouth
goes dry and this is why I open the latched
transom, again for you,
Moonflower, again.

In The Orangery

the color of heart beating / wild & jugular
trees like armchairs / naked & green /
pulled into / the shining /
eyes that blink / lashes like /
a darkened room / white blossomed /
me aching / aching / to be cloaked
in rind / skin over skin over pulp /
aching, aching / for the slow /
sticky / peel back / honeyfed /
bated breath / descent

False Jasmine

They say if you dream
of such blooms, it spells
good fortune in love.

Think *honey*.
Think *suckle*.

But what yellow
jasmine promises
(sweet, sweet nectar) —

it cannot provide,
turning toxic

the minute tongue
touches stamen.
Any honeybee

that lingers here,
corbiculae coated

in dusty pollen,
meets confusion,
double vision,

carries brood death
to the hive. Children

have died sucking
these tubes of plenty.
Why, is it when

you anther up, I part
my lips every time?

Persephone

I want to kiss your lips to stave off
the underworld,

to remain here on lush green earth.
I am tired of long journeys and dark tunnel

visions of men who want to possess me.
I am tired of death.

Your mouth is like fruit, like seeds,
like something growing, like pomegranates

split open, juicy, luscious—but Love,
even you are a slide towards the abyss,

even you lead me to lands
where nothing blooms.

Monotropa Uniflora

The ghost flower is "incapable of photosynthesis.
Unlike the green growing things around it, it can't
manufacture its own food but relies on symbiotic
relationships."

Marta McDowell,
Emily Dickinson's Gardens

She flecks with pink ownership
whenever anyone admires her translucence

(how pale! how delicate!)

preens a promise of perpetual sweetness —
but if plucked, she decays, blackens by the time

she's led home. She brings nothing to soil,
nothing substantially perlite is hers

in the garden bed. Instead, she feasts
off other hosts. Ghost flower, watching you
cling there hurts like glass

and reflects how often that which gathers
strength only from others

(how pale! how fragile!)

makes a darkness for itself
that is rootless.

Honeyfed

You kissed me against the lilac'd gate,
the scent so heady it attracted bees.

In memory I'm trapped inside this embrace:
you pushed me against the lilac'd gate.

The blooms so heavy they shaded your face,
in purple petals and darkened leaves —

You left me against the lilac'd gate,
your scent so heady it attracted bees.

The Crabapple in the Hollow

He left me here, so that green briar could grow over
 my bones, stiffen my limbs with sores. I had believed
in the songs he honed like they were gospel from the radio,
as if they came from a troubadour instead of a twice pawned
guitar. *My lover, I must have been dreaming all this.*
While I was sleeping, he brought his friends and danced
on my grave, spilling wine until the ground was soaked.
My bones were thirsty, so they drank—until all his notes
flowed out the holes. He sang how he loved me, how it
was only passion that made him rage, only the wild kisses
that led him astray. He sang his lies but when he wasn't
looking, I sprang, fully laden with red blossoms, ready
to tell the tale. I whispered it to anyone who might listen.
Some could not hear me; others looked up to see scarlet
spreading from the tree—and began to hum of ghosts.

Amanita

Destroying angel,
you look so familiar and benign

that one brings you
in with all

the common fungi
never noticing

that subtle difference
created by the membrane

covering
your skin's hide like an egg.

There now, volva—
left over at the base

of everything,
you broke the universal

veil in your upward
growth. Volva is also

a genus of sea snail
though that's not

relevant here
except to say you too are

a slug shaped
like a bullet

that rends the heart.

Water Hemlock

you, innocuous   /   smelling vaguely of dirt & carrot

white flowered   /   masquerading wild parsnip

you want me to   /   take you into myself

swallow   /   (without asking)

you whole   /   would be suicide

*

forgive   /   this refusal

(it's necessary)   /   to die in tremors

nauseous   /   to wake

to find gardens   /   amnesiac

overgrown   /   destroyed

The Lesson of Clematis

Honey, I tried to warn you that sometimes
what you plant for splendor (pretty color!)
turns invasive. In her thirst for sunshine,
Clematis crowds out every flower's
right to bloom. Don't revere the fairy-like
petalling; the joy of her traveling
is a ruse — she chokes her way to the light.
See how she meanders, unravelling.
You thought her yours, but those twisting
      tendrils
latch on where she wishes. Her agile growth —
her clever canopy — hides those she's killed.
You dither for this spectacle, false show.
She's called Devil's Mistress for a reason.
Careful. She blisters a gardener's skin.

Filtering Particle from Pain

Fire ants, like you, are architects
of mound making. They erect their red piles,
dot the lush green lawns with elaborate
structures that rise like oases in the humid air.
You'd think nothing would survive in
102-degree heat, 80 percent humidity,
but the ants bustle along, building
their fortresses of tiny granules. Fortitude
is something to admire. I know I should not
be tempted by the texture of cinnamon,
the color of curry—but the need to touch
the forbidden itches at my fingers. I could pick
you up like grains and sift you, ignoring
the sharp hot stings, pretending you are
harmless because you are miniscule,
insignificant. I could crush you
into nothingness, but not before my skin welts.

Ariadne Sends a Bouquet of Dandelions

On these yellow flowers, he was fed,
a brew to strengthen him to battle,
to brave our minotaur. Dear Phaedra,
I'll always be the one who led him out
of father's maze, red thread wound round
and round my ring finger.

You can't erase me, even with a curse. I was,
in fact, the first. Yes, you may remind me,
how he sailed away without a word, from Naxos.
And true, he married you instead —
but, sister, he's still sailing. What new seas
has he now discovered?
Above what sweet lips has he hovered?

I may have woken to disenchantment,
but I also woke to a better man, a god
who soothed the crying girl, lifted her
from the sand, and even now, eyes her over
the grapes at breakfast. So, go ahead,
and claim that throne. You still wander,
room to room, alone,

no true queen — just a second or third
happening. And your desperation's showing
plain as the grey streak in your hair. No wonder
your stepson hurries away from your glances.

And you should know, dear sister,
your fickle husband won't truck
good for goose, good for gander.

Mark my words, in this folly,
you'll lose. You can pull up all
of Hecate's weeds and blow your wishes
seed by seed to a thousand winds.
But you'll only find yourself deceived,
left with stems, and ragged leaves,
sharp as lion's teeth.

The Lesson of Aconite or Wolf's-bane

The curry killer killed her lover
               lacing dinner with poison
What part of her was howling
                     feed the wolf?

How loud it must have been to fly
to another continent and purchase
               bikh, *aconitum ferox*,
to fit her ferocity.
Did she think   *feed that wolf*

and his new bitch, younger & prettier,
and *not me, not me, not me?*

Did she think about how conscious
               he'd be, no one to save him
and his future bride,   just a sister
           dialing 999   too late?

Did he, in those last searing moments,
figure out how she let herself
               in with the old key and regret
               not changing the locks?

Did he wonder how—dizzy with betrayal,
               she didn't once think
of her own husband dying of cancer,
her children?   *Feed the wolf.*

Did he realize how the agile fingers
that once passionately stroked his abdomen,
         dusted the wolfsbane onto the curry?

How she howled from scorn   *feed feed feed*
as she sprinkled, thinking
         how he wounded her after sixteen years,
she should have known   he should have
known how cornered dogs bite,
         how beewolves sting.

Perennial

In speech, I steeple the church of empathy,
I steeple the church of forgiveness

I sepal the steeple to sprout lilies
of the valley, symbol of purity

and sweetness.
              They are deadly ingested.

Only in my poems do I tear you
apart   leaf by leaf   denude you
to stem. recognize that not all that's best
grows fair. I fight with it.

              Foul, this darkness.
This poison must go somewhere. I want to
lay it to rest, give it this dirt for tomb,
let worms pick it cleanbone—but I confess

it slithers back up, and always eludes,
over and over   regurgitating bloom.

Rue (The Thoughts of One Ophelia)

> There's rue for you; and here's some for me;
> we may call it herb of grace o' Sundays.
> —*Hamlet, Act IV*

Oh, my Grace. On Sundays,
you rule this,

> you make me
> rue all I have done.

> Midwife, supply me rue
> a way out of this
> supply me feverfew

> supply me licorice
> bittersweet
> thick blood come

Oh, my Grace,

> you make me
> rue all I have done,

falling knee
down before you, false
god of Gods. Me on
> knees and blushing up

Rule of Sundays
How you distort grace

and beget me
this rude awakening
at the Midwife's roost

God of Gods, you unmake me
every day I have been on
my knees and praying

blushing up, waiting
for some rogue awakening

And the Midwife gives me
supply of rue
for some bright flow
some red stain
against this whitening

If I had not looked
up to him as a god
for Gods, I would not

have gone down
knee to the ground

in supplication
how I rue letting him

rule my heart
false god of Gods
and I pray

supply me rue
a way out of this
supply me feverfew
supply me licorice
bittersweet

Oh, thick blood come,
please oh miracle
oh God,
undo, undone

Thoughts on Your Unweaving Me As
"The Unicorn in Captivity"

How could you so easily unravel this warp
and weft? The thread is pulled again
as you wander past my door, for the last time.
Gone is the horn of the unicorn, the forest floor
peppered in blossom. Gone tree, gone fruit.
Once you said you'd lay me down on a bed
of red rose petals. Cliché fenced me in.
Abandoned, petals dried to particle, crushed
dust and so it goes, the sleek white body of every
animal, the unspooled past, dissolving tapestry.
You glance at me, then shut your eyes, your tell
to a now boarded door. *Goodbye, goodbye.*
The hooves are disappearing, *Goodbye, body*
that shall love no more. Now the edge. Watch
the thread fall to the floor.

Ungardening

There are white flowers in my garden that smell
like menstrual blood.
                  They sear my head, crack
open pain against my temples,
        remind me of the white roses
                a boy brought once.
In the night, I awoke
             to breathe mummified petals.
Allergens, I learned, were potent, eternal.
I threw out both the blossoms and the boy.

When I discover the blood
          I'm not surprised. Every bloom
gets stained somehow; why shouldn't they bleed out?
When I realize   the truth—a cat
has found its prey—I blink, disturbed.
The branches shake, the dead bird   drops into
my hand. Its body scalds   my flesh,
     feathers   brushing my skin
like morticians' fans.   I tilt
the corpse to the brick walk,
         let the bones crunch.

Inside, the faucet water
         won't abate the burning,
and I stick my fingers
        and wrists into the freezer,
rest them against ice.   Here, I dream

of being frozen clean,   how wonderful
it would be to become   scentless, singular
          in a vase of Lucite, only appearing
to be water.   How wonderful
          to remain untouched,   no specks
of red staining   my white dress. I'm thirsty
          weeping over the fragility of bones,
I begin   to lick the cubes   to chill
 my tongue,   to stop the flow
of heat from inside me.

The Definitions You Taught Me

I make up new words every time
you disappear with your suitcase.
I spell them on the fridge with magnets:
iceloneliness, deepwoundly.
The black and white tiles lie stark
against the shiny surface,
as clear as a black pool. I see my reflection —
the movement of my fingers. I pluck and place.
I rearrange and rearrange
though I know no lexicon
will quench my thirst for sense.

You Didn't Show

After your birthday party, I gather the balloons
and slice their necks, let my own air back
into the room. All these molecules circulate
again and again like the rings of Saturn
in those old cartoons we watched in school,
the lights low. I still remember that cinematic
outline of a man drawing diagrams
on chalkboards—his squares & triangles
animating to form some dusty galaxy.
Do you ever think of him when you choose
to duck into the doorway of the next bar
to stare into the pooled whiskey in a shot glass?
Do you ever think of the infinite nature of space,
its black holes and nebulas, how they whirl
or do you just think of milk swirling in coffee
flavored liqueur? What do you think of
when you stay on the evening train, miss
your stop, leave me to maneuver around
the guests to look at the clock until
they apologize, pity-eyed, and shuffle out
like mourners for someone dead. In bars,
you're still alive, your mouth wide with pouring
words, your eyes twinkling like blue ice. I am
zombied in an empty, decorated, house
with a frosted sheet cake. Streaming news
does not report these kinds of accidents.
You are somewhere, tossing back another
and another and another and another, and I am
here trying to catch my breath as it is released
from its nylon casing.

Valentine Palindrome

From the back porch
where you've dumped the feathers and blood
in the trashcan

there, at the bottom
the valentine she made

the wife does not find
the silver dust

in the crack of the floor
the glitter does not catch

it is not found
this be-mine art

snap neck/bird wings/bone break

into the glass door
after flight
the cardinal does not crash

the construction paper stays
on the table
sticky with glue
against her fingertips
blue ink fails to smear

every clichéd rainbow decal does not peel

She is not fragile,
She does not expose herself
through its holes
an intricate lace doily heart
She is not making
a valentine
She is not giving you—

the birds, outside in the trees, singing.

Takoyaki

You and I are in the middle of the aquarium, escaping hot Monterey. "This cephalopod has escaped three times already," you tell me, squinting at small print. The octopus lounges on coral like a fat man on a towel. "Alrighty, then." I, too, have read the sign(s). I know that what is wandering is your attention. I'd like to add you may never be here again, at least not with me (but maybe with a redhead or a blonde, perhaps that girl with the dark hair that sways like an anemone). So, since this may be the last time, I want to see the dull colors of the starfish start to sparkle when wet: maroon to raspberry, burnt orange to tangerine. That's the way we were once— brighter and brighter—now the tide's gone out and soon, our apartment will be my own. Perhaps, someday, I may feel your tentacles on my bare ankles again and you'll draw me back, down under, and yes, I could pretend we'd be happy living in a glass bowl that is not ocean. But today, all I can say is that I know they fry those suckers up in oil in that little restaurant down the street—so maybe the next time the octopus escapes, they'll let it keep going.

Even Out Back, I'd Travel with a Trowel

Mambas move, bejeweled bangles in tall grass.
Though I've never been to Sub-Saharan Africa,

I know they're there. I've heard they drop
from the trees like unfurled tires spun

from semis. You make me think of them
when I look you in the eyes and you blink

poison. Mamba or rat snake, it's all the same:
what's prey to you, how you circle dreys,

and other safe spaces. I can pinpoint your slither
into sacred temples, your passage over cool

stone and while you might be blessed there,
I know these are not the gods I worship.

My mind keeps going back to the nest I found
this cold January: three small squirrels

spooning, deep sleep, dreaming, I know
you've got no scruples, you'll engorge

yourself, disregarding the soft fur and the quiet
breathtaking wonder of breath taken.

See, you squirm closer. See, you open your jaw
with needle bright bite. But imagine I strike

first—slit you down the middle, let you flip
headless in the death throes of your greed.

II.

Certain Bones, with Wisteria

- *The botanist Thomas Nuttall said he named*
  the genus Wisteria in memory of Dr. Caspar Wistar,
  friend of Thomas Jefferson.
- *In 2017, Sally Heming's quarters were discovered*
  at Monticello, adjacent Jefferson's, after having been
  turned into a men's bathroom in 1941.

In 1796, "certain bones" discovered in a field
are sent to the resident of the great house
with the pillars & portico.

   Think nickel. Think prestige.

      Outside, vines grow,
      their wood pale.
      The air is heady with the scent
      of purple blooms.

The great man in the great house
names the bones: *Megalonyx*,
a monument three times lion.

   Think discovery. Think pride.

      Wisteria can smell
      like heaven.
      Wisteria can choke
      like a disease.

He cannot believe in the mammal's extinction —
nature's inherent balance, he says —
Lewis & Clark can find it.

Think hubris. Think delusion.

> Some wonder if a woman
> loves the scent of wisteria,
> if the room in which she stays
> is still a prison

Lewis cannot find the "great claw,"
although he discovers many other things,
including several varieties of wildflower.

Think disappointment. Think open field.

> Years before, before the wife
> died, a promise
> like a choking vine:
> never remarry.

His friend analyzes the bones: discovering fossil
sloth not living lion. Caspar Wistar thinks
even the slothlike can be lion.

Think truth. Think exhume.

> The woman's room
> is easily reached.
> The woman's room
> is visited by the man.

Even the lion can be sloth. Jefferson
advocates for abolition but loses
over and over. He bends to public pressure.

Think difficult or think hypocritical.

> And the woman's fate is
> to be held
> The woman's fate is to be
> held down.

New discoveries are made all the time.
Two centuries later, scientists unearth
bright pterodactyl feathers.

Think gold & purple. Think remarkable.

> And the woman
> heals the sick.
> She is pregnant
> with generosity.

Two centuries later, the removal of a bathroom
floor shows a hidden room steps away
from the great man's bedroom.

Think bury. Think concealment.

> Many think it wise to keep
> wisteria contained. It can
> turn invasive & one must
> replant the entire garden.

What if the giant sloth were, too, the color
of wisteria? Could we see beyond the color
we imagine to the real thing?

Think dig, think excavation.

How many times did
the woman moan in her bed.
Six times, the woman
groaned in childbirth.

Wistar gives the ground sloth its name:
jeffersonai. What is the name for blindness
to a man you revere?

Think look away, look away. Or think ignorance.

She stays for the children
to be freed by the will.
The children freed by
the will of the man.

Wistar teaches anatomy, midwifery, surgery,
develops a set of anatomical models.
Promotes vaccines.

Think forefront. Think healer.

In the woman's room,
the man visits.
In the woman's room,
she prays through pain.

Later, Wistar becomes president of the Society
for the Abolition of Slavery.
Still later, Nuttall names his flower.

Think name. Think legacy.

Men receive their tributes
in bones and vines.
Wisteria climbs by twining
its stems into rope.

Names are emblazoned by those who write
history, by those who are given voice.
But we've always known—

Think secrets, think denial.

The flowers of some varieties
of wisteria are toxic.
Careful identification
is strongly recommended

Rumors in Richmond as early as 1802,
in neighbors' gardens. All men are created equal.
Except. . .exceptions become rule.

Think whisper. Think cover-up

Wisteria clambers
around any available
support. It's immensely
strong, wrist-thick.

Bones cannot stay buried though mislabeled
often and again and over. There is no safe passage
into locked rooms of defiant definitions.

Think reword. Think reevaluate.

Wisteria can be made to
twirl around latticework,
covering any wood, its scent
carrying through the air.

What can we know, what truth is evident?
What do we found, what do we find?
What was is reality like in the flesh of it?

Think private. Think unknowable.

Wisteria flowers can be made
into wine. If making tea,
use only blooms. The seeds
are poisonous.

Did she ever visit the bones of the man
after they lay underground, did she ever cast
blooms onto dark dirt?

Think forgiveness or think giant claw.

Wisteria vines can
collapse latticework,
crush posts, even
strangle large trees.

This plant that cloys, chokes, pokes,
creeps—it can bring the House down,
topple it to its rotting boards.

Think destroy. Think gone.

Ungarden the garden.

Till the soil, there can be
no recoiling. Every worm
is essential to the loam.

In the end we must build anew despite such
foundation. Monuments for the Sallys
and Marthas, the silent Harriets and Hesters.

Think haunt. Think repay.

The woman's body
breaks in chains.
The woman's chains
break from under blooms.

If purple petals dropped on these women's
faces when they lived —
our emblem should be the wisteria.

Think justice. At least, think recalibration.

Wisteria blooms
in clusters. It favors
fertile soil, deep
and rich. It grows.

Imagine monuments in this, our garden,
where men do not play snake.
Or judge in the rising after the Fall.

Think foundation.
Think bloom.
Think new world.
Think beautiful.

III.

High On Dopamine He Wants You Back

And he's convinced himself he can convince you.
　　　"Hey, baby, I'm the spark to ignite you."
You know now what you didn't know then.

Once you saw a stump in the Petrified Forest
on vacation with your family.
When your father smacked your mother
　　　for forgetting the map,
you learned to wander in and out of the trees,
cloud cover darkening every turn.
Later, cupping water over and over into your palm
　　　in a National Park restroom, you listened
to your mother weep behind a stall door.

You read the signs: *Only you can prevent forest fires.*

Only you. So you loved men who combusted,
spontaneously gave yourself to the flammable,
　　　stripped yourself bare for their ovens,
　　splayed yourself for their driptorches.
And burnt out, you can now tell that bastard
you're running outside to cover yourself with leaves,
　　his wood smoke skin can ash.

You've learned to love this new germination,
this prairie restoration. You've learned to love
the new taste of moss,
　　　　　damp dirt against your teeth.

Remnants of Tea Service

Saturday morning—years later, mind you—
I find, in the dustpan, a small sliver of china.
Brushed from the space between oven and floor,
a piece from the curved side
of the cup that used to rest in a matching saucer
on those other Saturday mornings, way back when.
It still shows part of a painted pansy:
That's for thoughts, my mother once said.
I hold, under my thumb, lavender traces of flower,
the exact color of the skin over my knuckles.

I had clung desperately
to the handle of that fragile thing
when you got up and said:
So long, nice to have known you,
and went out the back.
I heard your car door slam and the engine start.
I heard the rotation of the tires,
long after you were down the street.
I heard the swish of the clock radio's minute marker,
and the drip from the faucet,
as I stood there, clutching at sound and steam.

In case you didn't know, hot tea stains white walls.
The cup bounced—*unbelievable*.
It did not break until I beat it silly
with a frying pan.
I tossed the pieces in a garbage can

and they were gone forever, or at least
until, here—in the kitchen—
they shine under the fluorescent light,
bright and accusatory.

Puffing Up in the Apiary

you say, "You're a smacked beehive," a gibe
to disguise your own bad behavior, to hypnotize
me with blown smoke. Let me apologize,
but I'm not close to closing my eyes or excusing you.

Biting remarks skew or screw, right through
the center. It's true you only love this honey
when it's packed in pretty glass jars tied
with gingham ribbon. Any buzzing is betrayal

to you, even if bee is just being bee.
In your smacked up self-centered language,
bee is wasp is hornet is yellow jacket
so, let me see if I can put this in brackets,

for you, you don't need to shake [your racket]
at me to prove your ownership. Combing through
it all, down to the waxy bone, what's clear,
what's honed, is you're no one I'd call keeper.

Carp

Lotus seeds may remain viable
for as long as thirteen thousand years.
Roots to the bottom, the lotus sprouts
out of river soil to break the surface,
to spring pink into the air.
I swim in the muddy water of dark
attachment, pool in want and need.

The lotus unfolds its petals,
the expanding soul flowers.

I circle and circle the stalk
that leads to heaven, stir
the sludge of water. I cannot
tell what will sink and what
will rise from the murk.

I do not have that kind of time.

Thoughts on the Delivery of Your Dahlias

The silvered edge of the cardboard box
is reminiscent of coffin, of grandfather clock,
They lie there, feathered beauties.

Your ticking hiss has orchestrated
this last gasping symbol.
There's no shame in this ruin—

no need to explain my undoing
was by your little murder of crows.
Their deafening murmuration drove this

insanity, but there's no mistaking
your hand in it, your signature's apparent—
the looping capital offense.

Surely no petty reminder's necessary,
no need for perfumes and petals.
Nothing will ever permeate your aerated

bones, your substance's long gone,
decayed down to marrow.
You never were good at seeing tomorrow's

sunlight—how the cast of black
always shifts to burgundy, like wine.
I'm a little drunk I find, remembering

that this is just a passing fingering
of scars from the slices I cut to escape.
We were always as separate

as leaves, as distant as stars.
Such bouquets are no pity prize.
I will plant your every poison:

bury it, change it, reconstruct
its meaning. In the lexicon
of flowers, dahlias mean "to survive."

Here is the Blue Hydrangea

> "In Japan. . .an emperor supposedly gave hydrangeas to a
> maiden he loved as an apology for neglecting her when other
> business took up all his attention. . .Victorians were not as
> fond of the hydrangea. . .the flowers were sent to declare
> someone a boaster or braggart, or to chastise someone for
> their frigidity."
> — *thetsubaki.com*

Here you are, my former Adam,
iced down to the ground.

And still you burst forth, like bright
blooms reopening out of old wood—

blue as the color of swimming.
You're right, I cannot help temptation.

Yet, even reborn, you remain ingestible,
cyanide thriving in your petals.

You send bouquets to say you're sorry.
You send bouquets to accuse me of frigidity.

I can no longer decipher blue's true
symbol just the lawn's raw edge.

I've discovered I cannot make you less
deadly. I cannot keep you from rattling

me like a serpent. But if you will ask
me to throat your poison, if you want

me kept—a drowning Eve—
I will burn what's left and say:

I blacken your bloom, I refuse your seed.

This Uprooting Would Only Take Moments

fistfuls of green
pulled up like drowned

children. This uprooting
would only take moments

bulbs ungraved
to lie like skulls

It could be a blessing

       unless these flowers
       shrivel to reject replanting

       unless the roots curl up
       into the plant and deny

       new dirt, unless in weakness
       they call to aphids

       and infestation

but if this unrooting

is what is needed
this destruction

this risk. If this is what
is needed—this wasting

in order to no longer
be beholden, I will

plunge my hands wrist
deep—and wrench through dirt.

Tennessee Woodrose as Nimbus

I.

Here, in this dying garden, I till dry soil
over and over, heatblind & newly sobered
by abandoned hope.

What I mean to say is I can no longer wet
these brambles with my tears.
It's no use, there can be no harvest
with a ground festering: see how the worm eats
up from the root.
There's nothing left to do but put faith
in milky spore. Maybe pray.

II.

I don't know how to endure this decay —
do I pass through the gate, breathe the clearer
air beyond stone walls? Leave the infected? Die?

III.

Beyond the gate, the woodrose needs little
tending, its pink bloom unfolding
with unguarded glory against tumbled vine.
I could pluck the bloom for a crystal vase,
display it as mine.
I admit I ache for that ownership,
but any claim to that which grows of its own
accord, Love, is dangerous and deadly
(a worm is a worm is a worm).

IV.

I will not invest or infest.

V.

I brush lips to rosebud, and leave it, so that later
when I think of the touch, the blossoming thought
bursts to cover the cracked earth
of my tired plot. There is comfort in this end,
this freedom from tending,
this ungardening of seed,
the fine pink petals coming down like snow.

Bois d'arc

means "bow-wood," another name for Osage orange,
or mock orange   I suppose it's kind of a mock
to mistranslate—   names have meaning after all,
names are a call   but I keep thinking wood-dark
in my head, imagining what lurks unseen. Did you
know the Comanche used bois d'arc, in a watered
infusion of its roots, to cure afflictions of the eye?
I didn't and I wonder how they ground it down,
with what utensil? Then, could one see better,
in the dark wood-dark?
    Give me some. I'd try anything
    because I'm pretty lost here.
            Sometimes at night, a house
turns wood-dark and you must feel along its walls,
back from the bathroom   until it seems
you've gone too far,   out the patio door, into
forest   The Comanche used
bois d'arc for bows, hence bow-wood, & sometimes
I imagine arrows—   the lighted ones
from movies—flying through: a flame, a flare.
Daniel Day-Lewis is always behind them shouting
                I will find you
to Madeline Stowe.
    Sometimes, a stag stabs the moonlight
in a meadow, or the white wings of a barn owl
flap, or the warm yellow porch light draws me back.
    Sometimes, I go deeper in, even though
I'm afraid. My friend once said everything's better
if you can only take off your shoes. I haven't done so
since I was a girl, too much risk for cut or infection.

But what if I could traverse
this slippery moss of the riverbank, curl naked toes
over rock, dip my feet in, pale fish, under
the rushing water.   No one has ever held me
like these leaves, bowing down with their heavy
inedible fruit. I could juggle those, or chuck them
at the heads of my enemies—ghost figures that flit
through the dark while I listen for the call—survive,
I will find you—before I remember a film is just
a moving dream.   I do not know if I will be
found, or what fruit will be borne to me,
but perhaps there will also be true orange
or peach or plum, pulp over pit.

Fight or Flight

Twenty-dollar binoculars only let you see so far
and I'm straining here—leaning over the chair
in the upstairs room, parting the blinds with a finger.
I can't tell if it's an owl resting there in the dusk
or just a squirrel's nest, a mass of leaves and twigs,
slightly golden in the amber light.
The phone is ringing in the background
and I don't know if you're calling to apologize
or if the American Lung Society is asking
for money. I'm holding my breath anyway
as if not breathing (even inside the house)
will comfort the bird, will let it move naturally,
as if I'm not stalking the flutter of every feather.
Your voice on the answering machine is another call
on the wind, shaking dead leaves from branches—
I glance back quickly as if I could will silence.
Then, out the window, the mass unfurls, the talons
release the branch, the wings spread as the owl
reaches outward, flies into air.

Crisis, with Cassowaries

If you can kill two birds with one stone   let's have
a rock concert   and hang   the winged
creatures   that hover over our dirty laundry
          out to dry.   So you slept
     with her once and now you have thrown that
shuttlecock   into our game.   I could smack
it all down   with my racket.   The birdie
     would stick up,   stiff and yellow
from the green lawn.   Rigor mortis.

Hey, I have never believed   in Eden —
unless you count   the rainforest.   Even there,
bullet ants   could sting you to certain death,
          or snakes the circumference
of trees could choke the air from your lungs.

Cassowaries with heads   as bright as rainbows
          can open   your flesh   sharp and clean
as a hand-held   hole punch
     with one swipe of claw.

Once in grade school our teacher gave us black
construction paper to create a sky: the holes
          papered white behind
                to indicate intricate galaxies.

Really, if all we are is rocks ground down, why waste
our time being angry   when we can wash out
                    our spots and stains.
      The shirt still works   if you wear it close
                        with a vest.

My love, let's only symphony about the big things:
if we're bleeding, or punctured, or dying,
                        or lost.

Night Blooming Cereus After Desert Storm

We knew each other when we were children,
in a desolate desert town of barely 8000, where
water did not flow and wind whipped up red dust.

Years later, you served in a war where
the brown ground stretched for miles, kicking up
at the slightest motion. We hadn't spoken
since we stood under the disco ball
of a sixth-grade dance, squinting beyond corduroy
and glasses to true intentions. And yet,
you called me in your limited ration of long
distance—and drew portraits of me, sent them
carefully wrapped in tissue paper. Letters always
attached, though they weren't about love.
You wrote how IEDs and the fear of scuds

made sense, but the imagined sizzling sound
of a saw-scaled viper kept you up at night
as you lay on the hard ground and longed
for home. You were prepared for death,
but not from snakes whose snap seemed harmless
but could, days later, cause vascular coagulation,
heavy bleeding from several sites on the body.

When you returned from Kuwait that spring,
you flew to Michigan instead of heading home,

where the land was already dry and warm.
You said you longed for what was green.
The first night in my arms, you told me
of that fine film of dust that fell over you
one morning at four a.m., slowed your limbs
and your breath. You wept.

We lay in the soft grass of the yard
and counted stars, looked for Virgo,
we unbuttoned our clothes. What I offered you
was the only gift I had. I bathed you in the tub
and scrubbed your back, imagining
I could remove what was ingrained there.
I wasn't surprised by your absence
or the note you left behind.

You told me I made it hard to leave but I knew
it was a lie. For a long time, I imagined you running
through our dying hometown — past the oil derricks,
those long stopped sentinels, their paint peeling,
blown away by the wind — careening toward
the foothills, toward the seven-foot blooms of cacti
that only open at night, your arms extended
to embrace any kind of flowering that kept you
from remembering what unhinged its jaws at night.

The Saddest Girl You Ever Met

"But the *horses*," that man I used to know would say,
watching *The Misfits*. Those goddamn beautiful horses.
I tell my friend P how I hated the way
that man pretended he was sensitive to their delicate
nostrils' flare, to the way the sweat poured off
their flanks after heavy runs across open fields.

P. says, of course he was the type to keep replaying
some dead reel, enamored with an Old West
that doesn't exist except in mothballs
like John Wayne's hat in that antique store
in the middle of Universal Studios
where theme park stars walk fake sidewalks.

P. tells me I can love fake Hollywood but hate
the hell out of someone who pretends to care
for horses but is satisfied to see children
on the border shuffled into stalls to sweat and cry,
or when someone backhands a woman.

On the screen, I hear real Marilyn, screaming.
In black and white, her Roslyn flails in the flat land
punctuated by mountains and Guido tells Langland,
"she's crazy" as if that explains everything.
Call a woman crazy, and the conversation's done.

I tell P. that when fake cowboys search for Marilyn
on Google, the first thing they look for is "lost
nude scenes" because that's what they think
matters most about a dead blonde.
P. tells me they are beyond caring for luminous
flesh and sinew—she was no horse, after all.
Neither am I.

He was a man like that, P. says, a man
like that can't recognize a woman so close
to breaking. P. reminds me it's all right to survey
the scene and long to rewrite the lines in the desert
sand. P. reminds me it's all right to cry.

Unfettering Philomela

Bird, girl, you perch upon words
as if they were something solid

like trees instead of shimmering notes
of nothing. You have yet to learn

that whether they are kind or unkind
matters little. Betrayal is just an exposure

of rotted wood beneath auburn leaves.
Comforting nests, too, may only be

made of twigs. Storms blow things apart,
whether weak or well made. What have

you then—as you look outward to vast sky?
It is too simple to insist on you soaring

on wings magnificently unfolded—for yours
have been clipped and pinned. You're not sure

how they work. And so, I suggest you burst
into flame instead: regold your glory outward.

Become a purification of your own making,
a sharpening of beak, an opening of throat,

sing a keening or a calling, let it be yours,
and yours alone. Whatever cage they wish

to lock you in, whatever trap they've laid
or sprung, never let the weaving cease,

never let them hold your tongue.

Lesson of Fire and Phoenix

What boils down beauty is the cauldron
of odious comparisons
and the flaming conviction
you failed to brew the right concoction
      (that erstwhile love spell turnstile).

But damn toil and trouble—if you walk
away somnambulant, you leave the burners on.

Don't be a slow learner of the physics of scorching.
Don't choose to simmer like some shy incarnate.
Doubledown willingly. Own it, go for broke!

Hold open the oven door and throw your own
fool self in, devising the very worst hell of heat.

Succumb to all those imagined
defeats: melt, spill over, explode—
then navigate char. Rise, bare-boned,
purified, out of smoke.

Evolution

One:

    a. *Male moorland hawker dragonflies*
        are so eager to mate, they dive bomb
        ladies midflight. In defense, the latter plummet
        to earth, dead weight.
        This is not what happened to me.
        This is what happened to me.

Two:

    a. *Each time a female dragonfly mates,*
        she uses up a part of herself;
        multiple mating has no payoff for her.
    b. The man who would become my rapist
        taught me how to prep a pan for frying,
        rubbing oil and rag over aluminum.
        We kissed over the sizzle of chicken
        in the pan. We danced to music
        in the kitchen. He drew me in,
        circled warm, burners on.

Three:

    a. *n/a*
    b. It was a bait and switch. In advance,
        I told him what I wanted. I told him
        what I didn't want. When he did what
        I didn't want, I was sleeping, folded
        into myself. What he did was a violence
        without voice.

Four:

    a. *Dragonflies of this species*
       are approximately three inches long.
       The female has a brown abdomen,
       with yellow spots and a yellow costa,
       a vein that runs along the wings.

    b. I didn't even define the ochre ache
       on my arm until the silk fabric of my blouse
       made the color clear.

Five:

    a. *A female dragonfly lies still on the ground*
       as the male investigates, bursting to life
       only after he's flown safely out of territory.

    b. I would like to say I flew away but
       I hung on, diminishing after each flight,
       until I exploded in
       bluefire / wing / antennae / ash

Six:

    a. *Scientists say that females are learning*
       to adapt to lessen vulnerability
       to such harassment.

    b. My friend B. says we've all been there.
       Now, I am with a man not afraid to put
       his hands into cinder to phoenix me.
       He does not ask why I cannot
       cook the meat.

Seven:

     a.   *Many species of dragonflies are known to migrate. Though specific flight plans are often unknown, they have travelled extraordinary distances.*

     b.   This is not what happened to me. This is what happened to me.

Spell for Protection, with Lime

In a dream, my friend comes to me in a hazmat suit
carrying a lime, sucked out, the rind a rich

sad green stuck inside a sealed plastic bag,
which he holds out, tells me *it's a gift.*

Okay, I suppose—if one expects used fruit.
Awake, I discover that limes

"signify disaster, multiple failures" but may be
instead "new birth after strife," and I learn, too,

that sometimes limes can cause
phytophotodermatitis, a burning

that can scald a bartender's hands.
I'm in love with a bartender whose hands

magically soothe the customers with each
and every drink. I worry about all the touches

he gives away and all the touches he gets back.
It's a dangerous profession he's in. This world

doesn't treat magic well. My friend says *not to worry*
He says *everything will be okay, just don't unseal*

the bag. That's what he says in the dream
when he hands me the lime. He smiles

from the hazmat suit. I say *thank you.*
I take the plastic, I take the fruit.

Why Some Games Fall Out of Favor

Bob after apples, little children.
Remember to come up to breathe.
                              witches sink

eyes blurred by murk,
"scaredy-cat," bullywhispered
          clawsharp
into the ear
                    water dark
white limbs bouncing   against the washtub,
hair outward, octopudial in its tendrils.

                    the ankles tied
shiny orbs miss the expanded mouth
"Again! Again!" the children cry
                              stones press down
tart flesh of fruit
                    always drifts
                              out of reach
it cannot be gripped
                                        gasp
                    witches float
Come up for air!
          breathe, breathe, breathe

                    No juice
is worth drowning over.

Recovery like Budesonide

I.

Lilies, lilium, like valium, blur the senses

> He gave them in bouquets, pink stargazing
> blooms, the hems of the petals undulating
> as he held them out to me.
>
> > Only later did I discover his wife wore no. 19,
> > and that I was just another thing to bury
> > in flowers.

II.

Now is a slow unfolding, pulling back
        the coverlet and breathing
without pain, without the fear of the pollution,
        or perfume that thickens like fog
to swerve over the median of the throat,
        causing disaster.

III.

It's an interesting fact that stargazer
lilies were bred to gaze upward,
to bestow adoration.

> > Once, he pinned me to a bed, hands to
> > neck, wringing,
> >   bullysqueezing, so that more
> > than my saying what he wanted—

I surrendered to silence, to watch him
as if he were some vengeful god.

Witness the broken vases,
petals scattered at my feet

The option of taking in
anything but his rarified
atmosphere eliminated

IV.

Lilies are popular because nothing says
I'm sympathetic   to your ills like a scent
so rich it cloys the lungs.

Myth says Aphrodite at birth saw the lily
and jealous of its blank purity,
created the pistil
its fierce penetration upward
solely to damage the white surface.

V.

Please understand that
I could have lain there,
lined the broken bed with plastic.
I could have given myself to the wheezing,
insufflated to strawlike space.
Please understand how difficult it was
to gasp for any small pocket
of air,

to remove the idea of punishment
that I deserved the pistil,
that he was god

VI.

You do not need to know the story of how—
     what bones I broke to Houdini out.

You do not need to know how I broke the bloom
     off the stem. What whiteness I gave up.

VII.

Now I pray to the clean swath of sheet. My lips graze
fiber, mouthing over and over
     renew renew renew.
Watch me gulp the clean of cotton. Watch me buy
     fragrance free.

The Silver Birch

> "Everything is made out of Magic, leaves and trees, flowers
> and birds, badgers and foxes and squirrels and people. So it
> must be all around us. In this garden—in all the places."
> — *The Secret Garden*, Frances Hodgson Burnett

You've found me here, regrowing after the tragedy
of ash, from fire, regenerating the new green scalp

of bough. And though the bees hover at my
head even now, and I've survived in colder troughs

than this—so much feels gleaned and wasted.
I no longer know how to reach the sun.

Lore has always called me Lady of the Woods.
And a kindly boy once named me fairy,

replete with wings as sheer as gossamer.
I cannot accept that vision—you know I've been

brought down. The dirt under your nails proves you
know what you're getting into. Peel this bark;

it's paper thin. Discover the celadon skin coarsely
covered and the roots that still anchor in pliant

ground. I have so many dark fissures along my core.
Place your fingers to those sores and nurse

the delicate flowering leaves till they hang all over.
Then, on Midsummer's Eve, own them.

Place them above the door. Let me be the broom
that brushes evil from your floor. Let me be

the tea that banishes infection. Let me be
the landmark that guides you home

in the starless evening. Let me be your magic.
I realize I must have

been waiting for this. I have been praying a long
time for this. For you, Dickon, to Mary me.

Prayer for Hope, with Camellia

> The camellia was named after Georg Kamel (1661-1706), Jesuit
> missionary & naturalist. The Eighteen Scholars is a variation of
> *Camellia japonica*.

After the long winter, I visit the old house one last time. Ah,
Georg, I wonder what you would've thought if you knew of this
variety. What would the Eighteen Scholars have whispered to
you as you held the layers and layers of papery texture. Would
you have brushed the one-hundred and thirty petals to your
lips—or been transfixed by the holiness of symmetry? Would you
have cupped this heaviness in your hands and held it to your
heart, counted each section, beads of nature's rosary? If the red
camellia means love and the white means waiting, what can this
soft pink be but anticipation of a kiss. In distress, I offer up this
deepest plea. In fierce mourning, I ask to be held once like a
camellia. Oh, please murmur *thanks be to God, thanks be to God,
thanks be* and bless this fragile blossoming. I am not a Bohemian
but I ask you to crown my head with these roses of winter. Oh,
Georg, upon my head, bestow this

hanakotoba—
thanks be if only, you would,
oh, Georg—bless me now.

I Make Patterns So I May Believe in God

and so, when walking in a public garden
in Texas, I should not have been surprised

by a metal poppy the size of an umbrella
and how this took me back to stand

on a trail in California, following
my father's white legs up the hill

of wildflowers, the brilliant red
of poppies dominating the brush.

I am stranger in this foreign land
than I have ever been anywhere,

and this unexpected art in the middle
of the heat and azaleas is the first

familiar thing. This, and the small figure
my husband nearly mowed over in the yard

on my late father's birthday a month
before: a cheap plastic alien, holding

a birthday cake aloft. His grin
still clear on his blue face despite

waiting for me face down in the dirt
for who knows how long. I could

carry him in my palm, my fingers
uncurling like a flower at the beginning

of the day. The surprise of this tin
bloom = the blue alien = my father's

voice on the answering machine =
his silly joke, which took me years

to erase ringing out over and over,
= his *we must laugh and laugh*

at all this—quick, before we cry.

My Husband and I Talk of Nursing Homes
at the Shedd Aquarium

The great moray eel whips her head out
of the cave, demon-faced, cursing,
a prehistoric ghost.

Even with the glass between us, you pull back
from the glittering eye, the thirsty mouth,
this spectacle of ruined survival.

I want to say, *yes, death comes like this—*
powerful-jawed and unrelenting—
to remind us, by contrast, how fragile
the anemone is.

> Watch how it waves, tentacle-bright.
> That kills, too. Just in brilliant color.

Death always comes out stinging —
bite & poison, eel or flower,
disguised and hidden in the craggy reef.

I want you to know I see the coral
is the same color as the bedsheets
at the nursing home, the same color

as the scrubs of nurses who wipe your mother's
mouth and wheel her to Mass. And I want
to say, *yes, I, too, see her face in the moray's—*

the mouth gasping open and closed,
the trembling jaw that spells mortal.
We will all have our moment like hers,

where we will be spit out
     into that unfathomable blue.
The cave's invisible veil will float us
into primordial sea. But until then, slip

     back into the darkness with me. Hold
     my hand among all the glowing tanks,

all this breakable glass, hold me close
in the water until the inevitable last.

Countless Times, the Raspberries

Your parents are dying. Mine are already dead.
I have no words of wisdom, no comfort for loss.
It keeps coming and coming, sneaky bastard.

It pops up in songs and closets, in the curve
of the highway, in the shimmer of sun on a lake,
in spring, in old sweatshirts and the lost lace

of a shoe, white snake, crisp tulle, a ripped
seamed glove, the empty porch swing. You
cannot escape it. Not ever. And so, I offer

instead raspberries in a blue bowl. I offer
their miniscule seeds, the tart taste
and the green leaves, the name of Germanic

origin: Anglo-Latin *vinum raspeys*,
or from *raspoie*, meaning "thicket." I understand
grief as thicket—dense, unyielding. Once

in California, my mother and I picked the berries,
held them up as jewels and laughed. Her face
like a child's, bright wonder alive for a moment—

alive, alive— When the bees hum, I remember.
You will, too. Not much else is always.

Estate Sale

My body is an emptied house.
Here, you can cradle the soapdish of my skull.

There, my sighs stand among the dirty glasses
by the sink. My dreaming, tagged ceramic dogs

priced well over value. Here, are the clothes
I used to wear, rolled out on racks, on parade

with high heels and earrings and the buttons
you unbuttoned and the belts you unbelted.

I give up the red towels of my period, the utensils
of my knuckles, the garden hose of my psyche,

the books I read enlarged, the grey window shades
of my thinning hair, the necklace of my clavicle,

the flesh of my sorrow, the brown leaves of disease
floating on the surface of the swimming pool.

Love, when the gawkers have stopped
and the buyers have bought the remnants of junk,

close the door and roll up the rugs. And in the low
light, when it is just you and memory left, pull open

the cupboard and find the last tender vase
of my heart. Fill it with lilacs. Welcome spring.

Predictions

for Amanda Joyce

In some cultures, a rune—*a hlautlein*—
is marked with blood and thrown down like dice,
to prophesize fate. It is also true that people
in glass houses love throwing hard objects,
despite risk of cutting themselves, spilling
their own blood. We must be careful what magic
we practice, what heaven we intend
for ourselves or anyone else. Some gods don't
have our best interests at heart. Let us be mindful
of what is spilled or split, what broken mirrors
shard into the eye, heart. Restoration flitters,
arbitrary. What are we but bits of pebble broken
from a bag? What can be mortared back together
is often unclear, for what is magic without kindness?
How brave can we be when broken? This changes
the meaning of divination. Once, my friend rolled
over a hood of a car, hit windshield, struck
pavement—and did not lay still, but rose
like some sort of human miracle to take the hand
of the weeping driver and give the blessing
of forgiveness. Believe me when I speak
to you of the resilience of flesh and spirit. *Here. Now.*

After the Vineyard is Lost
for Audrey

When you have seen too much pain,
my daughter, lie down in the field at night
though it is scorched and smoke ridden.

I may not be there or I may be right next
to you, but you do not need me
to be whole or unguarded.

Breathe in so much beauty, the air
itself opiate. Let the wind kiss
your cheek raw with love.

Once on such a night you whispered
a secret: *our brain goes on even
when we are sleeping*, strange

comfort from your childish murmur.
Oh, my girl, I give these words back to you
to remember when you think

your heart is breaking. When the world goes
up in flame—even as the hot ash settles
to scar the skin—we *go on* in wonder,

blink at the new leaf, the green wood
visible beneath the bark of the vine,
the regeneration, the rarer fruit.

Tuck this knowledge
into yourself as talisman or prayer,
as bandage for burn.

Potential Tornado, with Backyardigans

On the long drive through Missouri,
wet summer air descending, she's watching
a DVD of five cartoon children (no, animals?
—no, children?—no, aliens?) dance
against grass so green it would taste
lime and her eyes are wide and happy
and she's singing, so that when, over her
head, I see the shape of cloud invert
to triangle, I singsong to you behind
the wheel *to your right, to your right,*
look to your right, aren't we having
so much fun, honey and you turn your head
and say, so calmly, "oh," and push
on the pedal and I think *why the hell did*
we drive but then again, planes fly into
buildings and mountains and she's only
three and then I remember worse statistics
about highway accidents and I'm thinking
what are you supposed to do in a situation
like this and I'm looking for an overpass
or a ditch and our girl is clapping and looking
at the beautiful screenworld and I'm thinking
don't let it lower don't let it lower, let us
slide through this divine space between
land and cloud (*we've got the whole wide*)
and in the distance there is a lightening
(*in our yard*) of dark cloud and you floor
it as if you are heading for home (*to explore*)
and I think *safety* and I think *thank you*
and I think *we are lucky*   (*see you next time*)

Texas February, with Yellow Flowers

After the snowstorm, we eat spice cake
off the Stangl *Fruit & Flower* plates
that were your mother's, exhausted.

Sun sparkles on snow. We have persevered.
The unlucky gardenias have turned black.
I know when pruned, their insides

will be brown. The azaleas have withered,
but articles on Google insist they'll bounce.
Our girl says we will always remember this:

the freak temperature drop, the sudden
loss of power, *The Trouble with Harry* cut off
just before the body's reburied, our own

stiff suffering under blankets and blankets
and layers of coats that we later consider
burning for the heresy of their worn familiarity.

This is not to say we didn't try to face it
in good humor, though on the fourth day,
the air below twenty, sobs choked our interior.

But now, *now*, the yellow of the kitchen
chairs, the lemon flowers on the dinnerware,
our faces turned like petals to the beams

of light. So much blooms in winter.
Restored, warmth creeps through us, hard
places turn soft again. I think of the Japanese

trio I read about once. We are like the Three
Friends: the pine, the bamboo, the plum
of our daughter between us. In these winds,

we bend rather than break, wintersweet.

Acknowledgements & Thank Yous

I am deeply grateful for the editors of these journals who had faith in my work and published variants of the following:

Alaska Quarterly Review:	Fight or Flight
Borderlands:	Persephone
Canary:	Carp
Channel:	Prayer for Hope, with Camellia; The Silver Birch
Cutleaf:	Lesson of Fire & Phoenix; Spell for Attraction, Containing Belladonna; The Sugared Plum
Crab Creek Review:	Valentine Palindrome
Fairy Tale Magazine	Unfettering Philomela
Future Fossil Flora:	If You Were to Change Me Into Flower
Ghost Town Review:	The Ungardening
Jabberwock:	Datura Innoxia; Perennial
Roanoke Review:	Lime;Sale Pending
MARY:	Ariadne Sends a Bouquet of Dandelions; Here is the Blue Hydrangea
Massachusetts Review:	Monotropa Uniflora
Mud Season Review:	Aconite, Amanita; False Jasmine; Puffing Up in the Apiary; Thoughts of You Unraveling Me As "Unicorn in Captivity"
Natural Bridge:	Takoyaki; Why Certain Games Fall Out of Favor
Normal School:	High on Dopamine; He Wants You Back
The Opiate:	Estate Sale; Predictions
Pedestal:	Recovery Like Budesonide

Plainsongs:	Even Out Back I'd Travel with a Trowel
Portland Review:	Remnants of Tea Service
Prime Number:	Countless Times; The Raspberries
Psaltery & Lyre:	After the Vineyard is Lost
Revolute:	Bois d'arc
Right Hand Pointing:	Definitions You Taught Me
River Styx:	Night Blooming Cereus; After Desert Storm
San Pedro River Review:	Filtering Particle from Pain
Southeast Review:	You Didn't Show
SWIMM everyday:	Thoughts of One Ophelia
Tar River Poetry:	Potential Tornado with Backyardigans
Vast Chasm:	My Husband and I Talk of Nursing Homes at the Shedd Aquarium
Waccamaw:	Crisis, with Cassowaries
Weave	The Crabapple in the Hollow
William & Mary Review:	Here Is The Green Apple, Water Hemlock
Yemassee:	I Hear You're Sick of Pomegranates

Several of these poems also appeared in the chapbook, *all breathing heartbreak*, from Dancing Girl Press in 2019.

I would like to thank the following for their help with this manuscript and my work in general:

I am very grateful to the editors at Fomite—Marc Estrin and Donna Bister—for their expansive support for this and other projects.

I thank all the girls (women) in the garden—but especially those near the *Gingerbread House*—M. E. Perkins, Tennessee Hill, Joy Clark, Kayla Haas, Jade Ramsey-Schlich, Arianna Lister, Sierra

Paige, Emily Townsend, Lauren Jeter, and M. Brett Gaffney—for inspiring and/or editing some of these poems. Thank you for reminding me blooming roses exist between the creeping vines.

For assistance in weathering the storm, I thank Andrew Brininstool, James Clark, Michael Given, Adam Greenfield, Joyce Johnston, Robert Paul Lamb, Michael Martin, Jeana Paul-Urena, Le'ann Solomonson, Bob Szafran, and Jerry Williams.

For reminding me the seeds I planted were only dormant and not lost, I thank: Linda Evan Autrey, Alison Baker, Jenae Batt, Tanna Burchinal, Tim Bryant & the Bosslight, Jane & Kyle Childress, Michael & Lisa Cocchiarale, Rob & Linda Rogers Davidson, Alicia Elkort, Nicole Ferrell, Anne Fleming, Lisa Fountain, Terri Hale, Matthew Ham, Tyler Heath, Patricia Henley, Joshua J. Hines, Ericka Hoagland, Gloria Hoefler, Michael Jaynes, Brenda Johnson, Jen Schomberg-Kanke, Aaron-Michael Kline, Kirstie Landry, Billy & Brittany Longino, Michelle Masterson, Amanda McMullen, Mahailey Oliver, Dylan & LaShanda Parkhurst, Dayna Patterson, Dan Paul, Ray Peterson, Matt Ramsey, K. Riley, Gennesis Roman, Camilla Saulsbury, Michael Sheehan & Mary Woo, Jim Smith, Liz Tasker-Davis, John Urban, Troy & Christina Varvel, and Lori Vaniece.

I am indebted to Mark & Kelly Staunton along with Michael S. Manley & Ronnie Craig, for being the Chicago center of my heart—and for my dear Maija, whose light will always shine—just now from a different desert.

Thanks to those always blooming inside the fence: Mike, Gina, Emily, & James, Nell, Julie & Gerry, Liz & Steve, Jim & Judilynn, and all the extended McDermott family. Also, no words of gratitude could ever express how Cornelia "Petie" McDermott changed and shaped my life and what it means to love, but I give them anway. I am blessed to have known her.

And most especially this book is dedicated to John & Audrey and our life at Three Bug Cottage. The bouquets are always for you.

About the Author

Christine Butterworth-McDermott is the author of two chapbooks—*Tales on Tales: Sestinas* (2010) and *All Breathing Heartbreak* (2019)—as well as the collections: *Woods & Water, Wolves & Women* (2012) and *Evelyn As* (2019). A former teacher, she now works as an writer, editor, and consultant. She lives in Texas with her husband, the writer John A. McDermott, and their daughter.

Fomite

Writing a review on social media sites for readers will help the progress of independent publishing. To submit a review, go to the book page on any of the sites and follow the links for reviews. Books from independent presses rely on reader-to-reader communications.

More poetry from Fomite...

Fomite

Kenneth Rosen and Richard Wilson — *Gomorrah*
Fred Rosenblum — *Playing Chicken with an Iron Horse*
Fred Rosenblum — *Tramping Solo*
Fred Rosenblum — *Vietnumb*
David Schein — *My Murder and Other Local News*
Harold Schweizer — *Miriam's Book*
Scott T. Starbuck — *Carbonfish Blues*
Scott T. Starbuck — *Hawk on Wire*
Scott T. Starbuck — *Industrial Oz*
Seth Steinzor — *Among the Lost*
Seth Steinzor — *Once Was Lost*
Seth Steinzor — *To Join the Lost*
Susan Thomas — *In the Sadness Museum*
Susan Thomas — *Silent Acts of Public Indiscretion*
Susan Thomas — *The Empty Notebook Interrogates Itself*
Sharon Webster — *Everyone Lives Here*
Tony Whedon — *The Très Riches Heures*
Tony Whedon — *The Falkland Quartet*
Claire Zoghb — *Dispatches from Everest*

For more information or to order any of our books, visit **fomitepress.com**

www.ingramcontent.com/pod-product-compliance
Lightning Source LLC
Chambersburg PA
CBHW030921140626
46545CB00016B/2337